'I like all simple things, boiled eggs, oysters
and caviare, *truite au bleu*, grilled salmon,
roast lamb (the saddle by preference),
cold grouse, treacle tart and rice pudding.
But of all simple things the only one I can eat
day in and day out, not only without disgust
but with the eagerness of an appetite
unimpaired by excess, is macaroni.'

From a short story, *The Hairless Mexican*
by W Somerset Maugham

# ANNA DEL CONTE'S ITALIAN KITCHEN
# LA PASTA

ILLUSTRATED BY FLO BAYLEY

PAVILION

First published in Great Britain in 1993 by
PAVILION BOOKS LIMITED
26 Upper Ground, London SE1 9PD

Designed by Andrew Barron & Collis Clements Associates

A CIP catalogue record for this book is available from the British Library

ISBN 1 85793 038X

Printed and bound in Italy by New Interlitho

2 4 6 8 10 9 7 5 3 1

This book may be ordered by post direct from
the publisher. Please contact the Marketing
Department. But try your bookshop first.

# INTRODUCTION

Pasta is the simplest food, even simpler than bread, consisting only of semolina and water for dried pasta and flour and eggs for home-made pasta. It is also the food that can change its character and appearance more than any other, like some great character-actor, assuming countless different roles. Think of the golden lightness of a delicate dish of tagliatelle with butter and compare it with the intriguing, exotic flavour of a green dish of spaghetti with pesto, or the rich earthiness of a dish of baked lasagne. All are equally good in their different ways, and pasta is the main ingredient of them all.

## TYPES OF PASTA

We Italians never look down on dried pasta. We consider it ideal for many sauces and would never regard it as merely a substitute for home-made pasta.

Factory-made **dried pasta** is made from durum wheat ground into semolina and mixed to a paste with water. The dough is forced through perforated metal discs to form the desired shape of pasta, and then dried. It should be buff-yellow, translucent and slightly shiny. The most common kinds of dried pasta are spaghetti, long pasta of various widths and lengths, shapes such as fusilli, conchiglie and penne, lasagne and small pasta for soups.

The '**fresh pasta**' sold in delicatessens or supermarkets is made with durum wheat semolina, flour, eggs and water. Though it is convenient, it certainly is not as good as home-made pasta, and it compares badly with dried pasta of a good Italian brand.

**Home-made pasta** has a lightness and delicacy that shop-bought 'fresh pasta' cannot match. So, when you want to make a recipe that calls for fresh pasta, do try to make it yourself, whether by hand or with the help of a machine. Remember, though, that it is not easy to make pasta by hand without practice, time and a long, thin pasta rolling pin.

Luckily there are good machines to speed up the task. Some electric machines make good pasta, but they are expensive, noisy and difficult to clean. The hand-cranked machines are cheap and easily obtained.

## THE COOKING OF PASTA

The time pasta takes to cook differs according to its quality and shape, whether it is fresh or dried, and, of course, personal preference. Even in Italy a plate of spaghetti that would be perfect in Naples might be considered undercooked in Milan. So I suggest you follow the table as a working guide.

## COOKING TIMES FOR PASTA

*Cooking time is calculated after the water returns to the boil*

| HOME-MADE PASTA | FRESH | DRIED |
| --- | --- | --- |
| tagliatelle | 1–2 minutes | 2–3 minutes |
| tonnarelli | 2–3 minutes | 3–4 minutes |
| lasagne | 2 minutes | 4 minutes |
| stuffed shapes | 5–6 minutes | 7–9 minutes |

*As you can see from this chart, home-made pasta that has been left to dry takes longer to cook, as does shop-bought fresh pasta*

DRIED PASTA

| | |
| --- | --- |
| capelli d'angelo | 5 minutes |
| spaghettini | 6–7 minutes |
| spaghetti, bigoli, long maccheroni, bucatini, linguine | 8–10 minutes |
| tagliatelle | 8–10 minutes |
| conchigliette or small tubular shapes | 8 minutes |
| gnocchi, ditali, orecchiette or any medium tubular shapes | 8–10 minutes |
| penne, rigatoni or any large tubular shapes | 9–12 minutes |

It is easy to cook pasta, but it can be spoiled by carelessness. Pasta needs to be cooked in a large saucepan and a lot of water – about 1 litre/1¾ pints for 100g/3½oz of pasta. Bring the water to the boil and then add cooking salt – about 1½ tablespoons for 4 litres/7 pints, which is the quantity needed for 300–500g/11oz–1lb 2oz of pasta. The water might seem too salty, but it is thrown away and is not absorbed by the pasta.

Slide all the pasta into the boiling water, stir with a wooden fork or spoon to separate the pasta shapes, and cover the pan so that the water returns to the boil as soon as possible. Remove the lid and adjust the heat so that the water boils briskly, but does not boil over. The pasta is ready when it is *al dente*, which means that it offers some resistance to the bite. The best test to see if the pasta is ready is to fish out a piece and pop it in your mouth. It is absolutely unnecessary to add cold water to pasta after cooking, as is sometimes suggested by non-Italian cookery writers.

## THE AGNESI METHOD

When I went to Imperia many years ago to see over the Agnesi pasta factory, the late Vincenzo Agnesi told me the way he liked to cook pasta. Here is what I call the Agnesi method, which I find more suitable when I have friends to dinner, since the pasta does not become overcooked if you leave it a minute too long in the pot. It also produces a dish of pasta that retains the characteristic flavour of semolina. The method is only suitable for factory-dried pasta.

Bring a large saucepan of water to the boil, add salt to taste and then add the pasta and stir. When the water has come back to the boil, cook for 1 minute, stirring frequently. Turn off the heat, put a turkish towel cloth over the pan and close with a tight-fitting lid. Leave for the same length of time that the pasta would take to cook by the normal method, i.e. if it were still boiling. When the time is up, drain the pasta.

## DRAINING PASTA

Pasta should be drained as soon as it is *al dente* (literally, 'to the tooth'): you must be able to feel its texture when you bite into it. However, if the pasta is going to be cooked further, by baking or frying, drain it when it is still slightly undercooked. Pasta for salads should be even more *al dente*.

It is important to drain pasta properly. Use a colander that is large enough to contain all the pasta you have cooked, and that has three little feet to stand on in the sink. Tip the pasta in, give the colander two sharp shakes, and immediately turn the pasta into a heated bowl or dish, into the frying pan with the sauce or into the saucepan in which it was cooked. (You can toss it better in the hot pan, with no worry about making a mess.) Penne, gnocchi or any shapes that are hollow need more draining because water may be trapped in the hollows. However, pasta should never be overdrained, as it needs to be slippery for coating with the sauce. Do not leave it sitting 'naked' in the colander, like the Chinese and Japanese do with their noodles. It should be dressed as soon as it is drained.

In southern Italy they do not use a colander for long pasta. The spaghetti is lifted out of the pan with two long forks. It is kept in the air for only a few seconds for the excess water to run off and then immediately transferred to the frying pan or the serving bowl. The Neapolitans say *'Gli spaghetti devono avere la goccia'* – spaghetti must be still just dripping.

# HOME-MADE PASTA

### MAKING THE DOUGH

200g/7oz, approximately, plain white flour (preferably Italian 00)
semolina for dusting
2 size-2 free-range eggs
*Makes about 350g/¾lb pasta, enough for 4 people as a first course or 3 as a main course*

*Note*: I recommend the use of Italian Grade 00 flour for making pasta dough. It is the best for this purpose because it absorbs the eggs more evenly, is easier to knead and roll out and, above all, makes pasta of a more fragrant flavour and a more delicate texture. Italian 00 flour is now available in most delicatessens and Italian specialist shops.

1 Put most of the flour on the work surface and make a well in the centre. Place the rest of the flour to one side. Break the eggs into the well. Beat them lightly with a fork for about 1 minute, then draw the flour in gradually from the inner wall of the well. I do this with two fingers because I find that gives me more control. When the eggs are no longer runny draw in enough flour to enable you to knead the dough. At this stage you might have to add the flour you set aside, and even a little more from the bag, which you should keep at hand. You should add enough flour so that the dough is no longer sticky. (It is not possible to give the exact amount of flour needed because it depends on the absorption capacity of the eggs and the humidity of the kitchen.) Work until the flour and eggs are thoroughly amal-

gamated, put the dough to one side and scrape the work surface clean. Wash and dry your hands.

*Note*: It is easier for a beginner to stretch a soft dough, though a dough that is too soft may stick and tear and become unmanageable. You can make a harder dough by replacing half the flour with fine semolina. This dough is difficult to roll out by hand, but it works all right in the hand-cranked machine. It makes a pasta that is less delicate and less smooth in texture, but with a definite flavour, particularly suitable for vegetable sauces.

**2** Proceed to knead the dough by pressing and pushing with the heel of your palm, folding the dough back, giving it half a turn and repeating these movements. Repeat the movements for about 10 minutes if you are going to make your pasta by hand, or 2–3 minutes if you are going to use a machine. Wrap the dough in cling film and leave it to rest for at least 30 minutes, though you can leave it for up to 3 hours, or even overnight.

### ROLLING OUT BY HAND

To roll out by hand you need, ideally, an Italian rolling pin, which is about 82cm/32in long and 3.7cm/1½in in diameter. If you do not have a *mattarello* – long, thin rolling pin – you must divide the dough and roll it out in two batches, so that the circle

of rolled-out pasta does not become too large for your rolling pin.

### ROLLING OUT BY MACHINE

I still think the hand-cranked machine is the best machine to use, and worth every penny of its very reasonable price. This is how to proceed.

Unwrap the dough and lightly dust the work surface with flour. Knead the dough, as before, for a further 2 minutes, then divide it into four equal parts. Take one piece of dough and carefully re-wrap the other pieces in cling film.

Set the rollers of the machine to the widest opening. Flatten the piece of dough slightly, so that it nearly reaches the width of the machine. Run it through the machine five or six times, folding the sheet over and giving it a 180° turn each time. When the dough is smooth, run the sheet, unfolded and without turning it, through all the settings, closing the rollers one notch at a time until you achieve the desired thickness. For good results it is very important that you push the sheet of dough through each setting. If the sheet tears or sticks to the machine, dust it on both sides with flour.

For tonnarelli (like spaghetti but square in section) stop the rolling out at the second from last setting. For tagliatelle or tagliolini stop at the last but one. For flat sheet pasta stop at the last setting. If the atmosphere is damp, dough rolled out too thin cannot be stuffed to make ravioli or other small shapes as, instead of drying, it becomes more and more soggy when filled with the stuffing. If you find this happening, stop rolling out at the last but one setting. Alternatively, I sometimes prefer to roll out the strip twice through the last but one setting. This makes the pasta just a little thinner, but not as thin as the last setting. Roll out the dough to the last setting only for lasagne or cannelloni.

### LONG PASTA, TAGLIATELLE, FETTUCCINE TONNARELLI, TAGLIOLINI

Lay each sheet of pasta dough on a clean tea towel, letting about one-third of its length hang down over the edge of the work surface. Leave until the pasta is dry to the touch and slightly leathery, but still pliable. This process takes about 30 minutes, depending on the humidity of the atmosphere and the texture of the pasta, and is essential because it prevents the strands from sticking together. Feed each sheet through the broad cutters of the machine for tagliatelle or fettuccine, or through the narrow ones for tonnarelli or tagliolini.

Separate the cut strands or wind them

loosely round your hand to make nests. Spread them out on clean tea cloths, and lightly dust them with semolina. Do not use flour, as this would be absorbed into the dough. The pasta is now ready to be cooked, or it can be dried and then stored in an airtight tin or plastic bag. Be very careful how you handle it because dried home-made pasta is very brittle and breaks easily.

### LASAGNE AND CANNELLONI

Proceed immediately to cut the shapes without drying the sheets. Cut each pasta sheet into squares of about 12 × 8.5cm/5 × $3\frac{1}{2}$in for lasagne, or 10 × 7.5cm/4 × 3in for cannelloni.

### PAPPARDELLE

Roll out each sheet of pasta to the last but one notch of the hand-cranked machine. Leave the sheets to dry for no longer than 10 minutes and then cut into ribbons about 12–15cm/5–6in long and 1.5cm/$\frac{3}{4}$in wide. Lay the pappardelle, not touching each other, on clean tea cloths.

### STUFFED PASTA SHAPES

You must work straight away while the pasta dough is still fresh and pliable. Roll out the dough and stuff the sheets, one or two at a time, depending on the shape being made. Keep the remainder of the dough in cling film.

Cook the little shapes straight away or leave them until the next day, spread out on a clean cloth, dusted with semolina. Once dry, you can store stuffed pasta in plastic boxes, in layers interleaved with greaseproof paper. Do not keep them for longer than a day or the stuffing might be spoiled.

### GREEN PASTA

The only coloured pasta I consider worth writing about is the traditional green pasta made with spinach. All the modern creations of red, black or brown pasta are gimmicks, and sometimes they spoil the flavour of the pasta. Flavour and colour should be added only by the sauce.

150g/5oz cooked fresh spinach, or frozen spinach, thawed and cooked for 5 minutes
225g/8oz plain white flour, preferably Italian 00
2 size-2 free-range eggs

Squeeze all the liquid out of the spinach with your hands. Chop it very finely with a knife. Do not use a food processor as the spinach would become like a liquid mass. Add the chopped spinach to the well in the flour together with the eggs, and knead and roll out as for normal pasta.

# SAUCES FOR SHAPES

In Italy there are said to be 350 different shapes of pasta (I've never counted them!). Although you are unlikely to find such a vast number of pasta shapes outside Italy, there are now a very considerable number to choose from. The drawings on pages 6–7 are of the most common and easily available shapes. In the recipes I explain which shape of pasta is usually dressed with the sauce in question, but you do not have to follow my suggestions slavishly.

There are, however, certain basic rules that govern which pasta shapes should be dressed with which sauce. In general, long thin shapes are dressed with an olive oil-based sauce that allows the strands to remain slippery and separate. Typical recipes are spaghettini with oil, garlic and chilli (page 20) and the spaghetti with tomato sauce on page 19.

Thicker long shapes, such as ziti, tonnarelli, bucatini or fettuccine, are best in heavier sauces containing prosciutto or bits of meat, cheese and eggs. A prime example is the carbonara on 37.

Medium-size short tubular pasta like ditali, orecchiette and fusilli are perfect with vegetable sauces of any kind, these being the shapes traditionally made in southern Italy where pasta is most often combined with vegetables.

Penne and maccheroni and other large tubular shapes, as well as home-made shapes such as garganelli and pappardelle, are the perfect foil for a rich meat *ragù* and for use in most baked dishes. A *ragù* bolognese is traditionally combined with tagliatelle, and the choice for a northern Italian pasta al gratin (page 48) is penne.

As for the proportion of sauce to pasta, an average of 2 generous tablespoons of well-reduced sauce per portion of pasta is a good general guide.

——— ARRANGEMENT OF RECIPES ———

The recipes in this book are grouped according to the main ingredient of the sauce. Thus tagliatelle with bolognese sauce will be found with other recipes whose sauces are based on fish and meat products, while penne with tomato sauce is with the other recipes for vegetable-based sauces, such as orecchiette with broccoli.

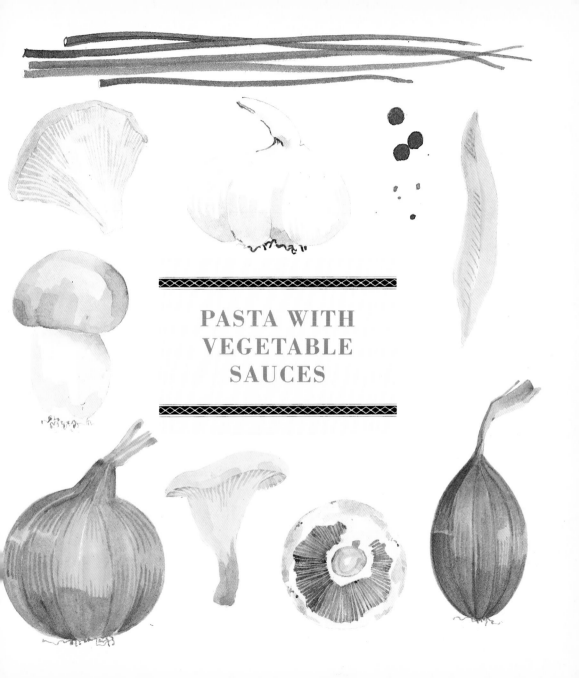

# PASTA WITH VEGETABLE SAUCES

# PESTO

PESTO SAUCE

30g/1oz pine nuts
90g/3oz fresh basil leaves
1 garlic clove, peeled
pinch of sea salt
4 level tbsp freshly
grated Parmesan
2 level tbsp freshly grated
aged pecorino
90ml/3fl oz extra virgin olive oil
40g/1½oz unsalted butter

Use young basil leaves for pesto; basil that has been growing for too long acquires an unpleasantly strong taste. The pine nuts must be fresh, i.e. of the current year, and the oil must be a very good olive oil, although an unassertive one. If possible use an oil from Liguria or from Lake Garda (they can be found in Italian delicatessens); they are less pungent than a Tuscan oil, and less herby than an oil from Apulia.

The oil must be added slowly, as for mayonnaise, so as to create the right thickness. Some cooks add walnuts as well as pine nuts, but I prefer to add only pine nuts in order to keep the emphasis on the fresh flavour of the basil. If you have time, make your pesto by hand in a mortar; more juices are released than would be by the chopping action of the metal blade in a food processor or blender. I add a little softened butter to the pesto just before serving, to make the sauce sweeter and more delicate. Before tossing the pesto with the pasta, always dilute it with 3 or 4 tablespoons of the water in which the pasta has been cooking.

1 Heat the oven to 180°C/350°F/Gas Mark 4. Spread the pine nuts on a baking tray and toast in the oven for 5 minutes or so. This will bring out the flavour of the nuts.

**2 To make in a mortar**:

Put the basil leaves, garlic, pine nuts and salt in the mortar. Grind against the sides of the mortar with the pestle, crushing the ingredients until the mixture has become a paste. Mix in the grated cheeses. Add the oil gradually, beating with a wooden spoon.

**To make in a food processor or blender:**

Cut the garlic into thin slices and drop them into the container of the food processor or blender. Add the basil, pine nuts, salt and oil and process to a creamy consistency. Transfer the sauce to a bowl and mix in the cheeses.

**3** Melt the butter over the lowest heat and blend into the pesto.

*Pesto freezes very well. Omit the garlic and the cheeses and add them just before you are going to use the sauce.*

# PICAGGE AL PESTO
## PICAGGE WITH PESTO SAUCE

In Liguria, the motherland of pesto, potato and a handful of French beans are cooked with the pasta. The pasta I like to use with pesto is picagge, a Ligurian word meaning ribbons. Picagge are half the width of lasagne, but the same length.

**1** Cut the pasta dough into strips about 5 × 12cm/2 × 5in. You can cut this shape as soon as you have rolled it out; you do not have to let the pasta dry.

**2** Cook the potatoes in their skins in boiling salted water. Drain, then peel and slice them. Put in a bowl.

**3** Top and tail the beans. Cook them in plenty of boiling salted water until tender and then drain. Add to the potatoes. Toss with 3 or 4 tbsp of the pesto.

**4** Cook the pasta in plenty of boiling salted water until *al dente*. Drain, reserving a cupful of the water, and return to the pan. Add 2 or 3 tbsp of the water to the pesto.

**5** Toss the pasta with half the pesto. Transfer half the pasta to a serving dish. Spoon over the potato and bean mixture and cover with the rest of the pasta. Spread over the remaining pesto.

*Home-made pasta keeps well in a hot oven for 15 minutes or so.*

Serves 4 as a main course

home-made pasta dough, made
with 3 size-2 eggs and
300g/11oz flour (page 9), or
500g/1lb 2oz bought linguine
or fettuccine
3 small new potatoes
225g/½lb young French beans
pesto sauce from the
preceeding recipe

# PASTA AL SUGO

## PASTA WITH TOMATO SAUCE

The first tomato sauce here is denser and darker than the second one because of the many sautéed vegetables. I like it best for dressing a dish of penne or bucatini, although it is suitable for most dried pasta.

**1** Sauté slowly the onion, carrot and celery in the olive oil until well softened (at least 10 minutes). Add the garlic and chilli just a few minutes before you finish the *soffritto* (sautéed mixture).
**2** Add the chopped tomatoes, the herbs and sugar. Season lightly with salt and pepper.
**3** Allow to simmer gently, uncovered, for 30–40 minutes, until the oil begins to separate out into small drops around the edge. Stir occasionally to prevent the sauce sticking to the bottom.
**4** Remove and discard the parsley stalks and the bayleaf, and push the sauce through the coarsest disc of a mouli. Put the sauce in a saucepan. When the pasta is nearly ready, heat the sauce.
**5** Cook the pasta in plenty of boiling salted water until *al dente*. Drain well and toss with the sauce. Serve at once, and hand round a bowl of freshly grated Parmesan.

A simpler and fresher tomato sauce can be made in the summer when good fresh tomatoes are on the market.

Peel, seed and coarsely chop 900g/2lb of ripe tomatoes and put them in a large heavy-bottomed sauté pan with 5 tbsp extra virgin olive oil, 6 garlic cloves, bruised, salt and freshly ground black pepper, a dozen snipped fresh basil leaves or $\frac{1}{2}$ tbsp of dried oregano. Cook briskly for 5 minutes, stirring frequently, until a lot of the tomato water has evaporated. Remove and discard the garlic before serving.

Serves 6 as a first course or
4 as a main course

1 medium-size onion,
very finely chopped
1 medium-size carrot,
very finely chopped
1 celery stick,
very finely chopped
4 tbsp olive oil
1 garlic clove,
very finely chopped
1 small dried chilli, seeded and
chopped (optional)
800g/1¾lb Italian canned plum
tomatoes, coarsely chopped
4 parsley stalks
1 bayleaf
1 tsp dried oregano
1 tsp sugar
salt and freshly ground
black pepper
500g/1lb 2oz tubular pasta,
such as penne or rigatoni
freshly grated Parmesan,
to serve

# SPAGHETTINI AGLIO OLIO E PEPERONCINO

## THIN SPAGHETTI WITH OIL, GARLIC AND CHILLI

Serves 4 as a first course or
3 as a main course

350g/¾lb thin spaghetti
(spaghettini)
salt
120ml/4fl oz extra virgin
olive oil
3 garlic cloves, sliced
1 or 2 dried chillies,
according to taste,
seeded and crumbled

This sauce differs from that in Tagliatelle with Butter and Parmesan (page 52), in a way that demonstrates the essential difference between the cooking of northern Italy and that of the South. The aggressive flavour of this dish shows all the characteristics of Mediterranean cooking, while the delicate, but certainly not bland, Tagliatelle with Butter epitomises northern Italian cooking with its abundant use of butter and Parmesan.

1 Cook the pasta in plenty of boiling salted water, remembering that spaghettini will cook in about 6 minutes.

2 Meanwhile, put the oil, garlic and chillies in a frying pan large enough to hold all the pasta later. Cook for 1 minute over low heat. As soon as the garlic aroma rises, the sauce is ready. Draw off the heat immediately or the garlic might burn; this would ruin the taste of the oil.

3 Drain the pasta as soon as it is *al dente*. Do not overcook it. Transfer the pasta immediately to the frying pan. Stir-fry for a minute or so, using two forks and lifting the spaghetti high into the air so that every strand is beautifully glistening with oil. Serve at once, preferably straight from the pan.

*No cheese is needed for this typically Neapolitan quick pasta.*

# PAPARELE E BISI

## TAGLIATELLE WITH PEAS

'*Paparele*' and '*bisi*' are the Venetian dialect words for wide tagliatelle and *piselli*, peas, which are one of the Venetians' favourite vegetables. Here they are used to dress fresh tagliatelle in a delicate, well-balanced sauce. The sauce is also suitable for dressing a dish of dried farfalle.

1 Put half the butter, the pancetta and the onion in a small saucepan and sauté until the onion is soft and golden.

2 Mix in the peas and the parsley and then pour over the stock. Stir and add salt and pepper to taste. Cover the pan and cook over gentle heat until the peas are tender. The sauce should be quite thin.

3 Meanwhile, cook the pasta in plenty of boiling salted water until it is *al dente*. Drain and return to the pan.

4 Toss the pasta with the rest of the butter, pour over the sauce and mix in the Parmesan.

Serves 6 as a first course or 4 as a main course

60g/2oz butter
60g/2oz unsmoked pancetta, chopped
1 tbsp finely chopped onion
300g/10oz cooked peas, or frozen petits pois, thawed
1 tbsp chopped fresh flat-leaf parsley
120ml/4fl oz meat stock
salt and freshly ground black pepper
home-made tagliatelle, made with 3 size-2 eggs and 300g/11oz flour (page 9), or 500g/1lb 2oz bought fresh tagliatelle
60g/2oz Parmesan, freshly grated

# ORECCHIETTE CON I BROCCOLI

## PASTA WITH BROCCOLI

Serves 4 as a first course or
3 as a main course

450g/1lb broccoli
salt and freshly ground
black pepper
350g/¾lb orecchiette or other
medium-size pasta, or
wholemeal spaghetti
2 garlic cloves, peeled
1 dried chilli, seeded
3 salted anchovies, boned and
rinsed, or 6 canned anchovy
fillets, drained
6 tbsp extra virgin olive oil
4 tbsp freshly grated
aged pecorino

The combination of vegetables and pasta has its origins in Southern Italy. In Apulia this broccoli sauce is always served with orecchiette, which means 'little ears' because of their hollow shape. Orecchiette are made at home there, with semolina, flour and water. They are now produced commercially by the best Italian pasta manufacturers and are generally available within Italy and elsewhere.

I find that this sauce, as well as being good with orecchiette, is also one of the few that can stand up to the nutty flavour of brown pasta made with wholemeal flour (a flavour of which, like most Italians, I am not particularly fond). Wholemeal pasta is made in a number of shapes, among which spaghetti is by far the most successful.

**1** Trim the broccoli. Divide into small florets and cut the stalks into 2.5cm/1in rounds.

**2** Bring a large saucepan of water to the boil. Add about $1\frac{1}{2}$ tbsp of cooking salt and then slide in the broccoli. Stir well and cook for 5 minutes after the water has come back to the boil. Retrieve the broccoli from the water with a slotted spoon and lay them on kitchen paper towels. Pat dry and set aside.

**3** Bring the broccoli water back to the boil and add the pasta. Cook in the usual way until very *al dente*.

**4** While the pasta is cooking, chop the garlic, chilli and anchovy fillets together and sauté them in half the oil for 2 minutes, using a large frying pan. Mix in the broccoli and sauté for a few minutes, turning constantly.

**5** When the pasta is done, drain and turn it into the frying pan. Stir-fry for a minute, then taste and check the seasoning.

**6** Before you serve the pasta, pour over the rest of the olive oil and mix in the pecorino. If you like you can serve a bowl of freshly grated Parmesan on the side, although I find that the pecorino gives the dish enough of a cheesey taste.

# TAGLIATELLE COL SUGO DI FUNGHI

## TAGLIATELLE WITH MUSHROOM SAUCE

Serves 6 as a first course or
4 as a main course

30g/1 oz dried porcini
450g/1lb mixed fresh
mushrooms: cultivated
mushrooms, oyster
mushrooms, brown mushrooms
(champignons de Paris)
75g/2½oz butter
4 shallots, very finely chopped
salt and freshly ground
black pepper
1 garlic clove, finely chopped
1 tbsp chopped fresh parsley
1 tbsp chopped fresh marjoram,
or 2 tsp dried marjoram
2 tsp tomato purée
1 tbsp flour
225ml/8fl oz meat stock
150ml/¼pt dry white wine
about ¼ of a nutmeg, grated
home-made tagliatelle, made
with 3 size-2 eggs and
300g/11oz flour (page 9), or
700g 1½lb bought fresh
tagliatelle
freshly grated Parmesan, to
serve (optional)

I have adapted an old family recipe to suit the mushrooms that are available in this country. Admittedly there are more and more species of mushrooms in the shops, but they are not equally available in all parts of the country. The other reason why I have adapted the Italian recipe is that the sauce is so good that I want to be able to make it at any time of the year, and not only when the wild mushrooms are in season.

The woody, leafy perfume of *ceps* is given here by the dried porcini (ceps), which you can easily buy in Italian delicatessens and many supermarkets. To these you add a selection of cultivated mushrooms for a sweeter flavour and for texture.

**1** Put the dried porcini in a bowl and cover with very hot water. Set aside to soak for 30 minutes or so and then lift them out. If they still have some grit, rinse under cold water. Dry and chop them. Filter the liquid through a muslin-lined sieve and reserve.
**2** Clean the fresh mushrooms by wiping them with damp kitchen paper towels. If they are very dirty, rinse them under cold water. Dry and chop them coarsely. (I use a food processor which I pulsate for only a few seconds.)
**3** Put half the butter and the shallots in a large sauté pan, add a pinch of salt and cook until the shallots are soft. Stir in the garlic and the herbs and sauté for a further minute. Add the tomato purée and cook for 30 seconds. Add the dried porcini, sauté for 5 minutes and then add the fresh mushrooms. Sauté over moderate heat for 5 minutes, turning the mushrooms over and over to *insaporire* – take up the flavour. Season with a little more salt and with a generous grinding of pepper. Turn the heat down and cook for a further 5 minutes.

**4** Melt the remaining butter in a heavy saucepan and blend in the flour. Add the stock, stirring constantly and hard until well blended.

**5** Heat the wine and add to the butter and stock mixture together with the nutmeg. Add some of the filtered porcini liquid, just enough to add mushroom flavour to the sauce, but not too much because it can be overpowering. Continue cooking very gently for about 15 minutes. Stir in the mushroom mixture. Check the seasoning and cook over the lowest possible heat for about 10 minutes.

**6** Meanwhile, cook the tagliatelle in plenty of boiling salted water until *al dente*. Drain, but do not overdrain, reserving a cupful of the pasta water.

**7** Turn half the pasta into a heated bowl and toss with half the mushroom sauce. Cover with the rest of the pasta and mix in the remaining sauce. If the pasta seems too dry, add 2–3 tbsp of the reserved water. Remember that fresh pasta absorbs a lot of liquid while it is sitting in the bowl. Serve at once with the optional cheese.

# PASTA WITH MEAT & FISH SAUCES

# TONNARELLI ALLA PURE DI TONNO

#### —— TONNARELLI WITH TUNA AND ANCHOVY PURÉE ——

Serves 4 as a first course or
3 as a main course

200g/7oz Italian or Spanish
canned tuna packed in olive oil,
drained
1½ salted anchovies,
boned and rinsed, or
3 canned anchovy fillets
3 tbsp pine nuts
3 tbsp freshly grated Parmesan
salt and freshly ground
black pepper
4 tbsp extra virgin olive oil
home-made tonnarelli, made
with 2 size-2 eggs and
200g/7oz flour (page 9), or
350g/¾lb bought fresh
tagliatelle

'There she goes again!' they say, when I hold forth about canned tuna. In most supermarkets the tuna on sale is skipjack tunny fish, an inferior fish, smaller in size and coarser in taste than the Mediterranean tunny. I strongly advise you to buy Italian or Spanish tuna packed in olive oil, which is available in most delicatessens. It is more expensive, but it is a very superior product. And it is absolutely necessary for this delicate creamy sauce.

Tonnarelli are a kind of square home-made pasta, particularly suitable for a smooth fish sauce.

1 Put the tuna, anchovies, pine nuts, cheese and pepper to taste in a food processor. Process while gradually adding the olive oil.
2 Slide the pasta into a saucepan of boiling water, to which only 1 tbsp salt has been added. (The sauce is quite salty.) Cook until *al dente*.
3 Scoop out a cupful of the pasta water and add about 6 tbsp of it to the sauce through the hole in the lid of the processor. The sauce should have the consistency of a thin béchamel. Taste and check the pepper.
4 Drain the tonnarelli and turn it into a heated bowl. Pour the sauce over it and toss thoroughly. Serve immediately.

# BUCATINI ALL'AMATRICIANA
## BUCATINI WITH SMOKED PANCETTA AND
### TOMATO SAUCE

A matrice is a town on the central Apennines where on 15th August huge cauldrons of this dish are prepared for the local *festa*. The sauce is traditionally made with pork jowl, and flavoured with a lot of dried chilli and grated pecorino to counterbalance the fattiness of the meat. In this country I use smoked pancetta which I buy in a thick piece.

1 Put the pancetta and the oil in a non-stick frying pan and sauté until the fat has run out of the pancetta and the pancetta is crisp and browned. Stir frequently.

2 Add the onion and a pinch of salt to the frying pan and sauté for about 10 minutes. Mix in the garlic and chilli. Cook for a further minute or so and then splash in the wine. Turn the heat up and let the wine bubble away to reduce it by half. Pour in the tomato sauce and simmer for 15 minutes to allow the flavours to combine. Add salt and add pepper to your liking.

3 Cook the bucatini in plenty of boiling salted water until *al dente*. Drain thoroughly, giving the colander a few sharp shakes so that the water trapped in the bucatini comes out. Transfer the pasta to a heated bowl and mix in three-quarters of the sauce and the pecorino. Toss very thoroughly and then spoon over the rest of the sauce. Serve immediately, handing round the Parmesan separately in a bowl.

Serves 6 as a first course or
4 as a main course

350g/¾lb smoked pancetta,
cut into 1cm/½in cubes
1 tbsp olive oil
1 small onion, very finely
chopped
salt and freshly ground
black pepper
1 garlic clove, finely chopped
1 dried chilli, seeded and
finely chopped
120ml/4fl oz dry white wine
450ml/¾pt tomato sauce (page
19, bottom)
450g/1lb bucatini
6 tbsp freshly grated aged
pecorino
freshly grated Parmesan
to serve

# TAGLIOLINI VERDI COL SALMONE E I FUNGHI

### GREEN TAGLIOLINI WITH A SALMON AND MUSHROOM SAUCE

**Serves 3 or 4**

20g/¾oz dried porcini
350g/¾lb piece of fresh salmon
250ml/9fl oz fish or
vegetable stock
120ml/4fl oz dry white wine
75g/2½oz unsalted butter
1 shallot, very finely chopped
salt and freshly ground
black pepper
180g/6oz cultivated fresh
mushrooms, cleaned and
coarsely chopped
1½ tbsp flour
3 tbsp double cream
home-made green tagliolini,
made with 2 size-2 eggs,
225g/8oz flour
and 150g/5oz cooked or frozen
spinach (page 9), or 450g/1lb
bought green tagliolini
bunch of fresh dill, chopped
freshly grated Parmesan,
to serve

In no way can I claim this to be a traditional Italian dish. It is an Anna Del Conte invention, good enough to pass on. It is definitely a *piatto unico* (one-course meal), with a good salad to be served afterwards, but not with it.

**1** Put the dried porcini in a small bowl and cover with very hot water. Set aside to soak for about 30 minutes.

**2** Meanwhile, put the salmon in a saucepan and cover with the stock and wine. Bring to the boil and boil for 1 minute. Remove from the heat and leave the salmon in the pan to finish cooking while you prepare the sauce.

**3** Put half the butter and the shallot in a heavy saucepan. Sprinkle with a little salt and cook gently until the shallot is soft, stirring occasionally.

**4** Lift the porcini out of the soaking water. If they are very dirty, rinse them under cold water. Dry and chop them coarsely. Filter the porcini liquid through a sieve lined with muslin to catch any grit, and reserve.

**5** Add the chopped porcini to the shallot and sauté gently for 5 minutes. Mix in the cultivated mushrooms, turn the heat up and cook until the liquid has come out of the mushrooms. Stir frequently.

**6** Lift the fish out of the stock and place it on a board. Strain the stock and reserve.

**7** Blend the flour into the mushroom sauce and cook for a minute or so, stirring constantly. Pour over a cupful of the fish stock and stir rapidly over very low heat until smoothly blended. Add the rest of the stock very gradually, stirring constantly. Add 2–3 tbsp of the filtered porcini liquid. The sauce should be quite thin.

**8** Bring the sauce slowly to the boil, then turn the heat right down, so that only a few bubbles break the surface of the sauce every now and then, and cook for 30 minutes. I use a flame diffuser. Alternatively you can cook the sauce in a bain-marie: place the pan containing the sauce in another saucepan of gently simmering water. You can of course simmer your mushroom sauce for only 5 minutes, but you will not achieve the same velvety, delicate yet rich sauce. At the end mix in the cream. Taste and adjust the seasoning.

**9** Skin and bone the fish and flake the flesh. Add to the sauce and keep warm.

**10** Cook the tagliolini in plenty of boiling salted water until *al dente*. Drain and return them to the hot saucepan in which they cooked. Toss with the remaining butter. Transfer to a heated bowl and cover with the sauce. Sprinkle the dill over the top just before serving. Pass the grated Parmesan round in a bowl.

# TAGLIATELLE AL RAGU
## TAGLIATELLE WITH BOLOGNESE SAUCE

Serves 6 as a first course or
4 as a main course

For the bolognese sauce
30g/1oz butter
3 tbsp extra virgin olive oil
60g/2oz unsmoked pancetta or
streaky bacon, finely chopped
1 small onion, finely chopped
$\frac{1}{2}$ carrot, finely chopped
1 celery stick, finely chopped
1 garlic clove, finely chopped
1 bayleaf
350g/$\frac{3}{4}$lb lean chuck or
braising beef, minced
1 tbsp tomato purée
150ml/$\frac{1}{4}$pt red wine
150ml/$\frac{1}{4}$pt meat stock
2 pinches of grated nutmeg
salt and freshly ground
black pepper
home-made tagliatelle, made
with 3 size-2 eggs and
300g/11oz flour (page 9) or
700g/1$\frac{1}{2}$lb bought fresh
tagliatelle
freshly grated Parmesan,
to serve

**B**olognese sauce is out of fashion. A great pity, although I quite understand why.

The early emigrants from southern Italy to the USA took their beloved spaghetti with them. In America, when they opened their restaurants, they realised that the locals were great meat lovers. Thus, instead of introducing spaghetti with the traditional tomato sauce, the Italians had the clever idea – financially clever, but not gastronomically – of serving spaghetti with a meat sauce or meat balls. The meat sauce was a watered-down version, both literally and figuratively, of the *ragù bolognese*.

It quickly caught on, and spaghetti bolognese became synonymous with Italian cooking. But in fact there is no combination of pasta and sauce that is less typically Italian!

In Bologna, *ragù* is used to dress the local pasta – tagliatelle, not spaghetti – fresh, home-made with eggs and local soft-wheat flour. And what a wonderful dish it is. If you cannot afford the time to make your own tagliatelle, choose good fresh pasta. Remember that dried egg tagliatelle made by a reputable Italian producer are often better than fresh pasta made with inferior flour, a minimum of eggs and a lot of water.

**1** To make the bolognese sauce, heat the butter and oil in a heavy saucepan and cook the pancetta for 2 minutes, stirring constantly. **2** Add the onion, and when it has begun to soften add the carrot, celery, garlic and bayleaf. Cook for a further 10 minutes, stirring frequently.

**3** Put in the minced beef and cook to brown it as much as possible, crumbling it in the pan with a fork. Do this over high heat so that the meat browns rather than stews.

**4** Add the tomato purée and continue to cook over high heat for a further 2 minutes. Still over high heat, splash in the wine and boil to evaporate. Remove and discard the bayleaf and pour in the stock. Season with the nutmeg, salt and pepper. Mix well and simmer, uncovered, for about 2 hours. Stir occasionally and add a little hot water if the sauce is too dry. The ragù should cook very slowly indeed, at the lowest possible simmer.

**5** Cook the pasta in plenty of boiling salted water. Fresh pasta cooks quickly, so stay around and test after $1\frac{1}{2}$ minutes. Drain as soon as it is *al dente*, reserving a cupful of the pasta water.

**6** Return half the pasta to the hot saucepan and stir in about half the *ragù*. Pour in the rest of the tagliatelle and the rest of the *ragù*. Mix very well, adding 2–3 tbsp of the reserved water if the pasta seems dry. Transfer to a heated bowl or deep dish and serve immediately, handing the cheese round separately.

# PASTA CON LE SARDE

## PASTA WITH FRESH SARDINES

Serves 4 as a main course

60g/2oz currants
6 tbsp extra virgin olive oil
1 red or Spanish onion, very
finely sliced
salt and freshly ground
black pepper
4 tbsp pine nuts
200g/7oz wild or cultivated
fennel leaves
2 salted anchovies,
boned and rinsed, or
4 canned anchovy fillets
450g/1lb fresh sardines, boned
(see Note opposite)
1 tsp fennel seeds
350g/¾lb bucatini

This dish from Sicily is like a history of that island in micro-cosm: part Greek, part Saracen, part Norman. The sardines and the wild fennel, typical food of the ancient Greeks, are here used to dress the most Italian of all foods, pasta. The dressing is lightened and made more interesting by the inclusion of pine nuts and currants, a Saracen influence, and the finished dish is cooked in the oven, a method brought to the island by the Normans. If you cannot get hold of wild or cultivated fennel leaves, use a small fennel bulb, cut into strips, together with its feathery green top.

1 Soak the currants in warm water for 10 minutes. Drain and dry well with kitchen paper towels.

2 Put 2 tbsp of the oil in a frying pan, add the onion and a pinch of salt, and sauté gently for 15 minutes, stirring frequently, until soft. Mix in the currants and the pine nuts and cook for a further 2 minutes.

3 Meanwhile, blanch the fennel leaves in a large saucepan of boiling salted water for 1 minute. (If you are using fennel bulb, cook until soft.) Lift the fennel out of the water with a slotted spoon, drain and dry with kitchen paper towels. Reserve the water in which it has cooked. Chop the fennel and add to the onion mixture. Cook over very low heat for 10–15 minutes, adding 2–3 tbsp of the fennel water whenever the mixture appears too dry.

4 Heat the oven to 200°C/400°F/Gas Mark 6.

5 Chop about half the sardines and the anchovies and add to the pan with the fennel seeds and a generous grinding of pepper. Cook gently for 10 minutes, stirring frequently and adding more fennel water whenever necessary. Taste and adjust the seasoning.

**6** Heat 2 tbsp of the remaining oil in a non-stick frying pan. When the oil is very hot, but not yet smoking, slide in the remaining whole sardines and fry on both sides for 5 minutes.

**7** Meanwhile, cook the pasta in the fennel water until very *al dente*. Drain, return the pasta to the pan and dress immediately with the sardine sauce.

**8** Grease an oven dish with a little oil and transfer the pasta to it. Lay the fried sardines over the pasta, dribble with the rest of the oil and cover with foil. Bake for 15 minutes.

*The dish can be prepared a few hours in advance and then baked for an extra 15 minutes to heat the pasta through.*

Note: To clean and bone fresh sardines, snap off the head of each fish and pull it away, thus removing most of the inside. Remove the back fin by pulling it off, starting from the tail end. Hold the sardine with one hand and open the belly with the thumb of the other hand, running it against the spine on both sides. Open the fish, butterfly-fashion, and pull the spine sharply from the head end towards the tail end, giving a last sharp tug to remove the tail. Wash and dry the boned fish.

# Pappardelle con la Lepre

PAPPARDELLE WITH HARE

Serves 5 or 6 as a main course

2 tbsp olive oil
75g/2½oz unsalted butter
30g/1oz unsmoked pancetta,
chopped
1 small onion,
very finely chopped
1 small celery stick,
very finely chopped
1 garlic clove, finely chopped
a small sprig of fresh rosemary,
finely chopped
the legs of 1 hare
150ml/¼pt red wine
2 level tsp flour
150ml/¼pt meat stock
salt and freshly ground
black pepper
pinch of grated nutmeg
2 tbsp double cream
home-made pappardelle, made
with 3 size-2 eggs and
300g/11oz flour (page 9), or
400g/14oz dried tagliatelle, or
500g/1lb 2oz bought fresh
tagliatelle

**O**nly the legs of the hare are used for this dish. You can roast the saddle as they do in Tuscany, which is where this dish originally comes from. It is a rich dish, and is regarded as a *piatto unico* – one-course meal – even in Italy, where pasta is usually only the first course.

**1** Heat the oil and half the butter in a sauté pan and cook the pancetta for 2 minutes, stirring constantly. Add the onion and sauté for a further 5 minutes, stirring very frequently. Add the celery, garlic and rosemary and cook until soft. Push the *soffritto* to one side of the pan.

**2** Add the hare legs and brown well on all sides. Raise the heat, pour over the wine and boil until the liquid has reduced by half.

**3** Transfer the hare to a plate. Stir the flour into the cooking juices. Cook for 1 minute and then pour in half the stock. Mix well. Return the hare to the pan and season with salt and nutmeg. Turn the heat down to very low and cook gently for a good hour, and the lid slightly askew. If the sauce gets too dry add a little of the remaining stock. The sauce should in the end be rather thick.

**4** Remove the hare from the pan. Bone the legs and cut the meat into very small pieces. Return the meat to the pan and add the cream and pepper to taste. Cook for about 2 minutes, stirring constantly. Taste and adjust the seasoning, then remove from the heat. Reheat the sauce before adding to the pasta.

**5** Cook the pasta in plenty of boiling salted water until *al dente*, remembering that if you are using fresh home-made pasta it will only take about 1 minute to cook. Drain and turn the pasta into a heated bowl. Add the remaining butter and spoon over the hot hare sauce. Serve at once.

# SPAGHETTI ALLA CARBONARA
## SPAGHETTI WITH EGGS AND BACON

The creation of this dish is attributed to the *carbonari* – charcoal burners – who used to make their charcoal in the mountainous forests of Lazio. Traditionally, the meat used was the jowl of the pig, but nowadays most carbonara is made with pancetta, which is belly of pork, similar to streaky bacon but differently cured.

Serves 3 as a main course or
4 as a first course

1 tbsp olive oil
4 fresh sage leaves
1 garlic clove, peeled
120g/4oz smoked pancetta or
smoked streaky bacon, cut into
matchsticks
350g/¾lb spaghetti
3 eggs
6 tbsp freshly grated Parmesan
salt and freshly ground
black pepper
60g/2oz butter

**1** Heat the oil, sage leaves and garlic clove in a large frying pan. Add the pancetta and sauté for about 10 minutes, until the pancetta is golden brown and the fat has run out. Discard the garlic and the sage.

**2** Cook the spaghetti in plenty of boiling salted water until *al dente*.

**3** Meanwhile, lightly beat the eggs in a bowl and add the Parmesan, a little salt and a generous amount of black pepper.

**4** Drain the pasta, reserving a cupful of the water. Return the spaghetti to the saucepan and toss with the butter, then add to the frying pan. Stir-fry for a minute or so.

**5** Remove from the heat and transfer the spaghetti mixture to a heated bowl. Pour over the egg and cheese mixture and add about 4 tbsp of the reserved water to give the sauce the right fluidity. Mix well and serve at once.

# BAKED AND
# STUFFED
# PASTA

# RAVIOLI DI PESCE

## FISH RAVIOLI

Serves 4 as a main course

For the pasta dough
200g/7oz white flour
(preferably Italian 00)
2 size-2 eggs
1 tsp olive oil
1 tbsp oil
90g/3oz unsalted butter
3 tbsp very finely cut fresh
chives
freshly grated Parmesan,
to serve

For the filling
60g/2oz unsalted butter
2 tbsp very finely chopped onion
300g/10 oz skinless white fish
fillet, such as Dover sole, turbot,
sea bass or sea bream
1 salted anchovy, boned and
rinsed, or 2 canned anchovy
fillets, drained
120ml/4fl oz dry white wine
150g/5oz fresh ricotta
4 tbsp double cream
3 tbsp freshly grated Parmesan
2 egg yolks
salt and freshly ground
black pepper

A new type of ravioli and a successful one. You can use any firm-fleshed fish including, of course, cod. The better the fish, the more tasty the ravioli!

**1** First prepare the filling: put the butter and onion in a saucepan and cook for 5 minutes, stirring and pressing the onion against the side of the pan to release the flavour.

**2** Meanwhile, cut the fish into very small pieces. Chop the anchovy. Add both to the onion and cook for $1\frac{1}{2}$–2 minutes.

**3** Turn the heat up and splash in the wine, then boil rapidly until it has totally evaporated. Flake the fish coarsely, transfer the mixture to a bowl and allow to cool for a few minutes.

**4** Add the ricotta to the fish mixture with the cream, Parmesan and egg yolks. Season with salt and pepper and mix very well. Set aside while you make the pasta dough, following the instructions on page 9, adding the olive oil with the eggs.

**5** Cut off one-quarter of the pasta dough, leaving the rest wrapped in cling film. Thin the dough down in the pasta machine notch by notch as far as the last but one notch, as described on page 11. If you are rolling out by hand, roll the dough out as thin as you possibly can.

**6** Work on one strip of dough at a time, keeping the remaining strips covered with a tea cloth. Place mounds of the filling about $\frac{1}{2}$ tsp each in a straight line along the length of the strip of dough spacing them about 4cm/$1\frac{1}{2}$in apart and the same distance from the one long edge. Fold the dough lengthways over the filling and, using a pastry wheel, trim the edges where they meet. Then cut into squares between each mound of filling. Separate the squares and squeeze out any air that may be caught in the ravioli. Seal them tight with moistened fingers.

**7** Place the ravioli on clean dry tea cloths, well separated. Cut off another quarter of the dough, knead in any trimmings from the previous batch and thin the strip down as before. If you are rolling out by hand keep the dough you are not working on well covered or it will dry up and become brittle. Continue making more ravioli until you have used up all the filling and/or all the dough. Leave the ravioli uncovered until they are properly dry; you can then cover them with another cloth.

**8** Bring a large saucepan of water to the boil. Add the oil and $1\frac{1}{2}$ tbsp salt. Drop the ravioli gently into the pan and bring the water back to the boil. Adjust the heat so that the water boils gently; if it boils too fast the ravioli might break. Cook until they are done, about 4–5 minutes, stirring gently every now and then. The best way to tell if they are done is to try one: the pasta should be still firm to the bite, *al dente*, at the edge. Lift the ravioli out with a slotted spoon and transfer them immediately to a heated and buttered bowl. Pat them dry with kitchen paper towels.

**9** While the ravioli are cooking, melt the butter in a small saucepan. Stir in the chives. Pour this sauce over the ravioli. Serve at once, handing round the grated Parmesan in a separate bowl.

# LASAGNE AL FORNO

## BAKED LASAGNE

Serves 4–6

home-made lasagne, made with
3 size-2 eggs and 300g/11oz
flour (page 9) or 700g/1½lb
bought fresh lasagne
Bolognese sauce
(page 32)
1 tbsp salt
1 tbsp vegetable or olive oil
75g/2½oz Parmesan,
freshly grated
15g/½oz butter

For the béchamel sauce
750ml/1¼pt full-fat milk
75g/2½oz unsalted butter
60g/2oz flour flavoured with
2 pinches of grated nutmeg

**F**ew dishes have been so badly copied abroad as baked lasagne, a dish that surely has acquired an appalling image. Yet when well made it is one of the finest creations of the very rich Bolognese cuisine. While I might occasionally be pushed to use shop-bought fresh tagliatelle, I find shop-bought lasagne frankly not good enough.

This is a party dish, perfect for a family celebration. A certain amount of time must be set aside to prepare it. So try to do it properly and make your own pasta. The difference is quite remarkable.

**1** If you are making your own lasagne, lay the pasta rectangles out, separate from each other, on clean tea towels.

**2** While the bolognese sauce is cooking, make the béchamel. You will find the recipe on page 48.

**3** Choose a large sauté pan. Fill it with water and add the salt and oil. When the water is boiling, slide in 5 or 6 lasagne at a time. Move them around with a wooden fork to stop them sticking to each other. When they are *al dente*, lift them out with a fish slice and plunge them into a bowl of cold water. Lift out, lay on cloths and pat dry with kitchen paper towels.

**4** Heat the oven to 220°C/425°F/Gas Mark 7.

**5** Butter a 30 × 20cm/12 × 8in ovenproof dish. Spread 2 tbsp of the bolognese sauce on the bottom. Cover with a layer of lasagne and spread over 2 tbsp or so of bolognese and the same of béchamel sauce. Sprinkle with a little Parmesan. Repeat, building up the dish in thin layers until you have used up all the ingredients. The top layer must be béchamel.

**6** Dot with the butter and bake for 20 minutes. Remove from the oven and allow to rest for at least 5 minutes before serving so the flavours can develop.

# IL RAVIOLONE

## PASTA AND SPINACH ROLL

Serves 6 as a main course,
8 as a first course

700g/1½lb frozen leaf spinach,
thawed, or scant 1.35kg/3lb
fresh spinach
salt and freshly ground
black pepper
3 tbsp very finely chopped
shallots
30g/1oz unsalted butter
225g/8oz fresh ricotta
90g/3oz Parmesan, freshly
grated
½ tsp grated nutmeg
1 egg yolk
home-made pasta dough, made
with 200g/7oz flour, the yolks
of 4 size-2 eggs and just enough
cold water to help the dough
absorb the flour (page 9)
4 large slices of unsmoked ham

For dressing the roll
90g/3oz unsalted butter, heated
with 1 bruised garlic clove and
4–6 fresh sage leaves,
or a thin béchamel sauce
(see Note opposite)
freshly grated Parmesan

In this dish the procedure for stuffing pasta is different. The whole sheet of pasta dough is rolled around the spinach filling. The roll is sliced when cold, just like a meat joint, and then heated up in the oven with its sauce. It results in a very attractive presentation.

**1** If you are using frozen spinach, cook the thawed spinach in a covered pan with a little salt for 5 minutes. If you are using fresh spinach, discard any wilted or discoloured spinach leaves and the tougher stalks. Wash it, and then cook in a covered pan with just the water that clings to the leaves and with a little salt for 5–8 minutes, or until tender. Drain the spinach, squeezing lightly to remove most of its moisture. Set aside.

**2** In a frying pan, sauté the chopped shallot in the butter over moderate heat. When the shallot turns pale gold in colour, add the spinach and sauté for 5 minutes, turning the spinach over and over to *insaporire* – take up the flavour.

**3** Transfer the contents of the frying pan to a food processor and add the ricotta, grated Parmesan, nutmeg, and, last of all, the egg yolk. Process for a few seconds. Check the seasoning.

**4** Roll out the pasta dough into as thin a sheet as possible, about 50 × 37cm/20 × 15in. Lay it flat in front of you. Square the sides to make a neat rectangle.

**5** Place the ham slices to cover the pasta rectangle completely, leaving a clean edge of about 2.5m/1in on all sides.

**6** Spread the spinach filling over the ham. Roll up as for a Swiss roll by first making a pleat and then rolling fairly tightly. Wrap the pasta roll tightly in muslin and tie the two ends securely with string.

**7** Use a fish kettle or other long, deep pan that can hold the roll comfortably and about 4 litres/7 pints of water. Bring the water to the boil, add about 2 tbsp of salt and then put in the pasta roll. Cook at a gentle but steady boil for 35 minutes.

**8** Lift out the roll. Unwrap it while it is hot and set it aside to cool, loosely covered with foil.

**9** Heat the oven to 200°C/400°F/Gas Mark 6.

**10** Cut the roll into 1cm/$\frac{1}{2}$in slices with a very sharp knife or an electric knife. (It is easier to slice the *rotolo* when cool.)

**11** Place the slices in a generously buttered shallow baking dish, overlapping them a little. You can dress the slices with either the garlic- and sage-flavoured butter and then a generous amount of Parmesan, or with a layer of Parmesan covered with the thin, well-flavoured béchamel. Cover the dish with foil and bake for 15–20 minutes. Remove from the oven and leave for 5 minutes before serving.

Note: For a thin béchamel, use 750ml/1$\frac{1}{4}$pt full-fat milk, 75g/2$\frac{1}{2}$oz unsalted butter and 45g/1$\frac{1}{2}$oz flour. Follow the recipe on page 48, heating the milk with 1 bayleaf.

# Pasta 'Ncaciata

### Aubergine and Rigatoni Cake

Serves 6 as a first course or
4–5 as a main course

2 aubergines, total weight about
450g/1lb
salt and freshly ground
black pepper
vegetable oil for frying
450g/1lb penne or rigatoni
60g/2oz butter
double quantity plain tomato
sauce (page 19 bottom)
225g/½lb Italian mozzarella
cheese, coarsely grated or
chopped
4 tbsp freshly grated Parmesan
4 tbsp freshly grated aged
pecorino
1 level tbsp dried oregano
2 tbsp dried white breadcrumbs

T his is a very showy southern Italian dish traditionally baked in a dome-shaped container, which can be tricky to unmould. In this recipe I suggest using a springform tin. It can be prepared a few hours in advance.

1 Cut the aubergines into 6mm/¼in slices. Place a board on the slant over the sink. Put layers of aubergine slices on the board, sprinkling each layer with salt. Leave to drain for 1 hour. Rinse thoroughly and pat each slice dry.

2 Heat enough oil in a large frying pan to come about 2.5cm/1in up the sides of the pan. The oil is hot enough when a corner of an aubergine slice dipped into it sizzles. Slide in a few slices of aubergine at a time and fry until deep golden on both sides. Do not overcrowd the slices or they will not fry properly.

3 Remove the fried aubergines with a slotted spoon, drain well and place in a dish lined with kitchen paper towels.

4 Cook the rigatoni in plenty of boiling salted water until very *al dente*. Drain and return the rigatoni to the saucepan in which they were cooked and toss with the butter. Mix in the tomato sauce, the three cheeses, oregano and pepper to taste. Check the seasoning.

5 Heat the oven to 190°C/375°F/Gas Mark 5.

6 Line the bottom of a 20cm/8in springform cake tin with aubergine slices. Fill in any gaps with cut-up pieces of aubergine. Line the sides of the tin with aubergine slices, cutting to fit. Place any aubergine left over on the bottom of the tin. Fill the tin with the rigatoni mixture and press down lightly. Sprinkle with the breadcrumbs.

7 Bake for 20 minutes or until the filling is hot.

8 Remove from the oven and run a palette knife around the side

of the tin. Place a heated round serving dish over the top of the tin and turn the tin upside down. Tap the base of the tin and give the dish a sharp shake or two. Unclip the ring and lift the tin away carefully. If necessary, press into place any pieces of aubergine stuck to the tin. Allow the cake to stand for at least 5 minutes for the flavours to combine.

LA PASTA

# PASTA AL GRATIN

**Serves 4 as a first course or
3 as a main course**

60g/2oz fontina, grated
60g/2oz Parmesan,
freshly grated
350g/$\frac{3}{4}$lb penne or maccheroni

For the béchamel sauce
750ml/1$\frac{1}{4}$pt full-fat milk
75g/2$\frac{1}{2}$oz unsalted butter
60g/2oz flour
salt and freshly ground
black pepper
grated nutmeg

Years ago, at the beginning of my married life in England, my husband asked me which was my favourite pasta dish. 'Very difficult question,' I answered. Recently, however, when he asked me the same question, I said, 'Pasta al gratin.' 'Oh really?' he said, and thought, 'What about that discerning palate she's so proud of?' But he was thinking of the macaroni cheese of his school days, and I was thinking of the velvety, cheesey delight of Pasta al Gratin.

Although it is made with a sauce with a French name, the dish is Italian. It is made in many regions, with certain variations. In the North, for instance, Parmesan is used, sometimes mixed with emmental or with fontina, as in my recipe, while in Naples a buffalo mozzarella is cut up and pushed here and there among the penne.

For all its simplicity, Pasta al Gratin needs a careful and patient cook, able to make a velvety béchamel and to drain the pasta at the right time, i.e. when still slightly undercooked, so that it can reach the right texture during baking.

**1** To make the béchamel sauce, heat the milk until hot but not boiling. Draw off the heat.
**2** Melt the butter, draw the saucepan off the heat and stir in the flour. Put the pan back on the heat and cook, stirring constantly, for about half a minute.
**3** Draw the pan off the heat and add the milk gradually. At the beginning add only a couple of tablespoons and incorporate well, before adding another few tablespoons. Adding the milk slowly in this way helps prevent the flour forming lumps. Return the pan to the heat and cook until the sauce comes to the boil. Season

with salt and pepper and with a generous grating of nutmeg. Cook for a few minutes, stirring constantly.

**4** To finish the sauce you can either use a flame diffuser under the pan, or you can put the pan into a larger saucepan of simmering water – the bain-marie method. Leave the sauce to cook very, very gently for 30 minutes; you only need to stir occasionally. This long slow cooking makes a rich velvety sauce that you would not be able to achieve if you only cooked the béchamel for 5 minutes, that is, just enough to cook the flour.

**5** Add the cheeses to the béchamel. Taste and adjust the seasoning.

**6** Cook the pasta in plenty of boiling salted water until very *al dente*. Drain thoroughly (penne tend to hold water in their hollows).

**7** Heat the oven to 180°C/350°F/Gas Mark 4.

**8** Coat a shallow baking dish (about 5cm/2in deep) with a little of the sauce. Dress the pasta with about two-thirds of the béchamel and transfer to the prepared dish. Spread the rest of the sauce all over the top. Bake for about 30 minutes, until the penne at the top begin to brown.

**9** Leave out of the oven for 5 minutes before serving, to allow the flavours to blend while cooling a little.

GRAN
MUGNAIO

Spadoni

ACETO

METODO LENTO A TRUCIOLO

Leonardo Spadoni

0.50ℓe    7.45%

# OTHER FAVOURITES

# TAGLIATELLE AL BURRO E FORMAGGIO

## ———— TAGLIATELLE WITH BUTTER AND PARMESAN ————

Serves 4 as a first course or
3 as a main course

home-made tagliatelle, made
with 2 size-2 eggs and
200g/7oz flour (page 9)
salt
60g/2oz Parmesan,
freshly grated
60g/2oz best quality unsalted
butter

In my home in Milan when I was a child, special butter was used for this sauce. The best farm butter was sold, cut in pieces and wrapped in muslin, by the best delicatessen in Via Monte Napoleone. And the tagliatelle were, of course, home-made.

This recipe is characteristic of northern Italian cooking. It is also the dressing used when you are lucky enough to have a white truffle to shave over it. To do the dish justice, you should make your own pasta and buy the best unsalted butter, as well as making sure your Parmesan is a proper Parmigiano Reggiano, of which you grate an ample quantity just before serving.

**1** Cook the pasta in plenty of boiling salted water until *al dente*. Drain – but do not overdrain – and turn half the pasta into a heated serving bowl. Add about 4 tbsp of the cheese and stir well. **2** Cut the butter into small pieces and add half to the bowl. Toss thoroughly, then add the remaining cheese. Add the remaining butter and toss until all the butter has melted. Serve at once.

*In Milan, more cheese is handed round separately in a bowl.*

# TAGLIOLINI PICCANTI FREDDI

## TAGLIOLINI WITH A PIQUANT SUN-DRIED
#### ———— TOMATO SAUCE ————

I do not usually like cold pasta, but I make a few exceptions. This is the best cold pasta dish I know, and it has always been a great success at my demonstrations.

When I have not got time to make my tagliolini, I prefer to use a good brand of dried tagliolini such as Cipriani or Spinosi, rather than shop-bought fresh pasta.

For this recipe buy loose sun-dried tomatoes that you reconstitute, not the kind under oil.

———————

**1** To reconstitute the sun-dried tomatoes, put them in a bowl. Heat 200ml/7fl oz of water with the wine vinegar, and when just boiling pour over the tomatoes. Leave to soak for at least 2 hours.
**2** Lift the tomatoes out of the liquid, lay them on a wooden board and dry each one thoroughly with kitchen paper towels. Cut them into thin strips and put in a bowl large enough to hold the pasta later. Add the oil, chillies, garlic and basil.
**3** Cook the tagliolini in plenty of boiling salted water. Drain it when it is even more *al dente* than you would like for eating it hot. (Overcooked cold pasta is really unpleasant.) Turn the pasta into the bowl and toss very thoroughly, lifting the strands up high so as to separate them. Leave to infuse for 2 hours or so, then fish out the garlic and discard. Scatter with the olives and serve.

Serves 4 as a first course

180g/6oz sun-dried tomatoes
120ml/4fl oz wine vinegar
6 tbsp extra virgin olive oil
1 or 2 dried chillies, according to taste, strength and size, seeded and crumbled
5 garlic cloves, bruised
a dozen fresh basil leaves, torn into small pieces
300g/11oz dried tagliolini, or home-made tagliolini made with 2 size-2 eggs and 200g/7oz flour (page 9)
salt
75g/2½oz black olives, such as Kalamata

# TAGLIARDI E ZUCCHINE AL SUGO DI PISTACCHIO E BASILICO

### TAGLIARDI AND COURGETTES WITH A PISTACHIO NUT AND BASIL SAUCE

Serves 6 as a first course or
4 as a main course

home-made green pasta dough,
made with 3 size-2 eggs,
350g/¾lb flour
and 225g/½lb cooked spinach
(page 9), or 250g/9oz bought
green tagliatelle or tagliardi
200ml/7 fl oz extra virgin olive
oil, preferably from
Sicily or Puglia
4 garlic cloves, bruised
600g/1¼lb courgettes, cut into
matchsticks
salt and freshly ground
black pepper
120g/4oz shelled pistachio nuts
50g/1¾oz fresh basil
30g/1oz fresh flat-leaf parsley
15g/½oz unsalted butter

L ast year, during a short visit to Sicily, I had more interesting pasta dishes than during many a year in London. The pistachio and basil sauce was prepared for a dinner in the garden by Vittoria Spadaro, a friend and a good cook who is passionate about the great tradition of her island's cooking. The combination of flavours and the presentation of this dish epitomise the very best of Sicilian cooking.

The pasta used by Vittoria was green pappardelle which she made herself. If you do not have the time or inclination to make your own pasta I suggest you buy a box of the excellent tagliardi made by Cipriani, available in the best delicatessens. It is the best egg pasta on the market. It has a delicate silky texture which is normally found only in home-made pasta. Cipriani pasta is expensive, but when cooked it grows in volume more than any other pasta. And it is so good that it is well worth its higher price.

1 If you are making your own pasta, roll it and cut into pappardelle (page 12). Spread the pasta out on clean tea towels while you make the sauce.

2 Heat 2 tbsp of the oil and the garlic in a non-stick frying pan. When hot, add the courgettes and fry at a lively heat until golden all over. Shake the pan very often. They are ready whey they are tender, not still crunchy but not yet soft, and when the flavour has fully developed – about 15 minutes. Season with salt and pepper.

3 While the zucchini are frying, put the pistachios into a small saucepan. Cover with water, bring to a boil, and boil 10 seconds. Skin the pistachios, taking them out of the hot water a few at a

time for easier peeling. Dry them thoroughly and put in a food processor.

**4** Rinse and dry the basil and parsley and add to the pistachios. Process while adding the rest of the oil through the hole in the lid. Stop the machine, push the mixture down from the side of the bowl, and process again a few seconds. Add salt and pepper to taste. Scoop out the mixture into a serving bowl and place the bowl in a warm oven.

**5** Cook the pasta in plenty of salted boiling water until *al dente*. Drain, reserving a cupful of the pasta water, and turn immediately into the heated bowl. Add the butter and toss very thoroughly, adding 3 or 4 tablespoons of the reserved water to give the pasta the right fluidity.

**6** Spoon the zucchini and their juices over the top of the pasta and serve at once.

# CONCHIGLIE DI RADICCHIO ROSSO COL RIPIENO DI PASTA

—————— RED RADICCHIO LEAVES FILLED WITH PASTA ——————

1 garlic clove
2 salted anchovies, boned and rinsed or 4 canned anchovy fillets, drained
1 dried chilli
4 tbsp extra virgin olive oil
salt
225g/½lb ditali or gnocchi
4 outside leaves from a large head of red radicchio
freshly ground black pepper (optional)

Although I am not very keen on pasta salads, I am not as hostile towards them as one woman evidently was, judging by a recent report in *The Times*.

'Laurette Bruson threw macaroni salad at Richard, her groom, during a tiff at their wedding reception in Tampa, Florida, and he responded by shooting her with a .22 pistol.'
This salad is an attractive dish, definitely not for throwing, with the shiny ditali tasting mainly of olive oil. I use a peppery oil for this dish, such as an extra virgin oil from Chianti or a fruity and herby oil from Sicily or Puglia.

If you cannot find a large radicchio head, use a Webb's or a round lettuce.

———————

**1** Chop the parsley, garlic and anchovies and put them in a large bowl together with the whole chilli. Beat in the oil and add salt to taste.
**2** Cook the pasta in plenty of boiling salted water, remembering that cold pasta needs to be more *al dente* than hot pasta. Drain, refresh under cold water and drain again thoroughly. Pat dry with kitchen paper towels. Turn the pasta into the bowl with the dressing and toss well. Leave to infuse for about 2 hours.
**3** Wash and dry the radicchio leaves thoroughly and lay them on individual plates.
**4** Fish the chilli out of the dressing and discard. Taste and add pepper, if liked. Fill the salad leaves with the pasta just before serving.

# LIST OF RECIPES